INVISIBLE *Chains*

Discovering the freedom of God's grace

Invisible Chains
by Kerrie Oles and Olivia Womack

www.myinvisiblechains.com

Published by HeartSpring Media
P.O. Box 1655 • Keller, Texas 76244
(817) 431-1405

International Standard Book Number
(ISBN) 978-1-5869505-1-4

Library of Congress Control Number: 2009934105

Printed in the United States of America

Cover design and book layout by SeedStudios.com
Creative Director: Russell Lake

Contents

Invisible Chains

This book is dedicated
to my Lord and Savior, Jesus, the lover of my soul.

In the book of Leviticus 25, this law of God was given:
If a man sold his inheritance and he had a near
kinsman who was willing and able, that kinsman
could buy back his brother's lost inheritance.

I was unknowingly selling my inheritance,
day by day, but my kinsman came and
bought back all that I had lost…

He redeemed my life and this book is for Him.

In the midst of my own life, I found myself. In most places of the world, I am considered ordinary. God called my name, formed me in the darkness of my mother's womb, and brought me into existence.

This is my story that recounts my life of 13,680 days prior to understanding that every life is valuable, including my own.

Kerrie Oles

Introduction

THE SET UP

Joe Womack, a former pool hustler and loner, smelled of cigarettes, smoke, and stale beer. He wrestled with his conscience all day while playing pool. Should he or shouldn't he go on the blind date. *This shot will determine if I go or not,* he thought. *With low left-hand English on the cue ball, I can sink the nine; win the game and the fifty dollars.*

He took careful aim, a soft level stroke, and the ball rolled into the pocket with the finesse of a pro shooter.

He could afford to buy the stranger dinner now, but that wasn't part of the plans, just drinks and dancing. His friend, David, a real prankster, had made the date arrangements with Olivia, and she sounded too good to be true. "I swear I'll get David for this if she turns out to be a real loser," he mumbled under his breath. Joe collected his winnings, pulled the crumpled directions to the girl's house from his pocket, and headed for a new adventure.

Oh well, we'll see what happens. Who knows she might be the love of my life. he thought, starting his cherry–red corvette.

Walking up the steps to Olivia's house, he felt he had done enough preparation for the loser date by merely sliding into his holey jeans and fake leather coat.

Olivia had spent a fortune getting ready for the mystery date. She'd had highlights added to her hair, bought a new dress, and purchased the most expensive shoes she had ever owned. A matching coat and gold necklace completed her ensemble. Turning to check the final results in the full–length mirror, she dabbed Gardenia perfume behind each ear, and flipped a thumbs–up to the attractive reflection.

Out of the dating scene for over a year, at age twenty, she was a devastated divorcee. She vowed never to trust another man. He certainly had to be the exception, but she wasn't looking to find a father figure for her son this night. She just wanted a grown–up conversation with someone who had a three digit I.Q. and a pulse. She hoped this someone might make her smile again– if only for a night.

Joe rang the doorbell. He decided if an ugly girl answered the door, he would explain that Joe couldn't make the blind date, that one of his two sons was sick. That sounded reasonable. She'd believe that excuse. He buttoned his jacket, cleared his throat, and rehearsed his explanation.

Olivia opened the door, smiled, and stepped into Joe's heart.

The ex–professional boxer was quick on his feet, but he was knocked out by the vision that stood before him. With chin on his chest, in awe, he managed to mumble his first words to her, "I'm going to marry you."

Did he just propose? She didn't even remember his last name. Forget the three digit I.Q. What a moron.

After ten months of dating, Olivia found her smile again, and said "I do". A pre–made blended family was created. Three years later, the odd couple became my parents.

The Pig Arrives

When I was born, a month early, weighing in at four–and–a–half pounds by C–section, I started crying in the womb; the embryonic fluid damaged my trachea. My breathing came in sounds of a pig's grunt. My mom thought she had given birth to a pig. With every inhale and exhale, I made annoying grunts every minute of every day until I was the age of two.

Mom wanted to shelter me from prying eyes and nosy people. Surely she wanted to leave me in the car when she ran errands, but since this is illegal, she took me with her in public and braced herself for unwanted comments.

We lived in a small, rural Oklahoma town with lots of well-meaning ladies to tell her, "Honey, do you know your baby is – well, sounds like she's choking?"

Mom wearied of hearing that comment. "Nah, that's just the way she breathes," she'd respond flippantly.

Obviously Mom was a little spunky. She tried to protect me even though we became the talk of the town.

It's ironic that I had tears in my mother's womb, because most of my life has been filled with tears that damaged more than my trachea. I loathe saying that because my mom is amazing, I love my father, and I have a beautiful life now. I never had a broken bone or surgery of any kind. However, through stormy voyages in life, I became enslaved and walked with emotional limps…limps caused by invisible chains that eventually crippled and blinded me. I didn't know a ransom had already been paid.

I lived shackled with life's *invisible chains.*

Man is born broken. He lives by mending.
The grace of God is glue.
Eugene O'Neill

Chapter 1

THE EVENT

Why do most days start with an intrusive beeping alarm clock? Time schedules. Responsibilities. I slapped the noisy beeper and hit the snooze button. My husband kissed me good morning, and we snuggled in the warmth of our bed. Too soon the irritating alarm chirped again. If only the alarm clock had had a "cancel-the-day mode."

Phillip went about his morning ritual. He sat on the side of the bed, yawned, stretched, and rubbed his eyes. He had worked sixteen hours a day for several weeks on a new client's presentation. "Yes," he answered my question before I spoke. He knew me too well. He read my mind.

"What?" I flipped my hair over my shoulder with an attitude.

"You know I have to go to L.A. I know you hate for me to go out of town, but it can't be helped."

I pulled on my comfy, tattered robe and sauntered into the kitchen, half mad at him. Why did he have to always be right? The automatic coffee pot sputtered its last gurgle. Thankful for the hot liquid, I blinked blurry eyes and hoped the caffeine would give me the jolt I needed to shake off my headache. Reaching for my favorite coffee mug, I couldn't grasp the handle. My eyes wouldn't focus.

"That's weird," I mumbled to the elusive coffee cup.

Phillip pulled on the untied belt of my robe. "What's weird, honey?"

"Oh nothing," I needed his strong arms to hold me. I turned to hug him, "just a thought. Don't worry about me. I'm fine. I just miss you already."

"Kerrie, things will be fine while I'm gone." He stroked my back. "As usual, honey, I'm running late. There's a Starbucks at the airport. I'll pick up a muffin and coffee when I get there." He kissed my ear and tried to step back to wait for my worry list of "what ifs" to start. He'd lived this scene a thousand times before.

"I hate to be alone."

"With you gone that means three nights alone, just me and the boys. What'll I do if the car won't start?" I squeezed him tighter so he couldn't pull away. "Or one of the boys gets hurt or puts a toy in the toilet and it backs up?"

"Call a doctor, a plumber, or your dad," he said a little out of sorts with a shoulder shrug. "You know the importance of this presentation. Now I have to go. Love you." He gave me a peck on the cheek and closed the back door with a soft thud.

Alone in deafening silence.

I hate to be alone.

"Maybe more caffeine will jump-start my energy," I said to the closed door. Was it my imagination, or did the room do a 360 degree spin? Maybe I turned too quickly. I poured a cup of coffee and pulled open the kitchen medicine drawer. I stirred things around until I found two capsules for my headache and some eye drops. *These will make me feel better*, I assured myself.

"Da Da," Cameron's sweet baby voice floated onto the air via the baby monitor. My one–year–old was awake. Morning had started.

"Mommy, Cameron woke me up."

"I know, Caleb," I called to my four–year–old. "I'll turn on the TV. You come downstairs and watch cartoons while I get your brother up. Then I'll start breakfast."

"I want happy face pancakes."

"Okay," I agreed and smoothed his top–knot cowlick down with the palm of my hand. "I guess I gave up my corporate job to be a chef of happy face pancakes just for you."

"Did you really, Mommy?" His gorgeous blue eyes sparkled up at me. "You're the best mommy in the world."

"I want banana eyes and chocolate chips for the smiley mouth. Okay, Mommy?"

"All right, all right, I'll fix you what you want. Mom's don't have time to feel bad," I grumbled climbing the stairs. *Wish my world only consisted of that kind of worries.* With two hungry boys to feed and loads of clothes to wash and fold, my usual busy day began.

By noon, most of my motherly tasks were completed, but my headache pounded to the beat of a hundred-drum band. My eyes watered and blurred worse by the second. Needing a shoulder to cry on, I took a few minutes to call my mom. I described, for thirty minutes, how I felt in detail. We decided I was a tired, overworked mother of two and a nap was the prescribed medicine.

"Call me later," Mom said and hung up the phone.

At four o'clock, I awoke to unbearable throbs. I rummaged through the medicine cabinet like a person on a two-month fast in search of a chocolate bar. Finally, I spotted a half-bottle of cold medicine, swigged down several gulps, used the back of my hand to wipe my mouth, and brushed tears away.

Kerrie get control. Crying will only make your eyes worse and your head hurt more. What is wrong with me? I grabbed the countertop to keep from falling. The room became a tilt-a-whirl ride. I swirled into a bottomless black hole.

Something was rocking me back and forth. "Mommy, Mommy," Caleb pressed his nose against mine, "why are you sleeping on the floor?"

Floor. Why was I on the floor? How long had I lain there? I rubbed the back of my sore head. My lips felt numb. I whispered in slow motion. "Get Mommy the telephone."

"But Mommy, you said to never play with the telephone."

"It's okay. Mommy needs to call Nanny." Soft shuffles crossed the ceramic tile.

"Here, Mommy. Can I talk to Nanny?"

Both of us needed my mom.

He placed the phone into my hand. My fingers glided along the touch pad. I hoped I had hit redial. *Four rings. Please be home.*

"Hello."

"M–mom," I stuttered. "I–I need you and D–Dad. I can't see…I can't see…everything is black and fuzzy, and I think I fainted."

"Do I need to call an ambulance?" Mom tried to mask the panic in her voice. "It'll take us thirty minutes to get there in the traffic."

"No, I don't think so. Please, just come now. Quick as you can." I hit disconnect and hoped whatever was wrong would disappear as quickly as it had come over me. With Phillip away in L.A., I couldn't be alone with the boys.

Thank God for parents. I felt like the little boy who cried wolf. Heaven only knows I've cried wolf hundreds of times, but this time I truly needed them – and now.

My legs felt wobbly like rubber bands. I knew I shouldn't try to stand.

"Mommy, why are you crawling like Cameron. Are we playing horsy?"

"No!" I snapped, and hoisted myself onto the couch.

Poor Caleb, He didn't understand what was happening. Neither did I. *Had time stood still or flown by? Is this the way you feel after you faint? Are you in a gray, blurred fog? I must stay calm.*

Frozen to the couch, I dropped one foot to the floor to stabilize myself. My fingernails dug into the sofa cushions. The slightest movements turned the room into an out-of-control merry-go-round. Thirty minutes. An eternity. *Oh please hurry, Mom and Dad, hurry.*

Finally, the key rattled in the front door lock. Help had arrived.

"Kerrie," I heard Mom say from the darkness. "I'm here. You're all right. There's nothing wrong with you. Remember, you're all right." She stroked my hair and repeated the words over and over. What was wrong with her? Was she trying to reassure herself or me? I didn't understand her statements.

Something was definitely wrong.

Fear mounted within me.

Poor mom was needed in two places at once. I wanted her with me at the hospital and to stay home with the boys. After a few moments of debate, Dad spoke with a voice of authority. "I'll take you to the hospital. You know I don't cook and I won't change a diaper." There, the decision was made. I knew that Dad disliked hospitals. Throughout my life, I was very aware that he loved me, but he's not the nurturing kind. The gentle kind of dad who caresses your cheek and tells you everything is fine. In the past, I ached to be the kind of little girl who could sit on her daddy's lap and be comforted. That never

Fear mounted within me.

happened; I wasn't another strong son for him. A fault I couldn't correct.

My dad was born in the midst of the Great Depression era to poor farm people. He plowed fields behind a team of mules, picked cotton by hand, and milked cows daily. He lived a tough life – making him a macho kind of man. To me, he seemed harsh and distant…too busy, like every man I loved. Even now, Phillip was busy in L.A. – the story of my life. God himself was probably too busy to deal with my problem.

When you have nothing left but God, then for the first time you become aware that God is enough.

Maude Royden

Chapter 2

THE LONG RIDE

My dad's Impala sped toward the hospital. The car was filled with silence. Tires hummed a pavement tune. Dad had no words of encouragement and felt helpless. So did I. Out of the darkness, my dad's rough hand patted my arm, a giant show of affection on his part. Fear closed my throat. I squeezed my eyes shut. *Don't let him see my weakness.* He could not and would not handle tears. Tears weren't an option. If I cried, I'd be his four–year–old little girl again, afraid in the corner. Let me be strong like one of his sons.

The car stopped in front of the emergency room entrance. "Can you make it inside by yourself? I'll park the car." This translated: I'm not coming inside with you. I wasn't surprised, just terribly disappointed. Didn't he believe me? I couldn't see; I was blind.

"My heart raced like a long-distance runner."

I bit my lip and groped for the car's door handle. Instincts kicked in. With outstretched hands, I found a wall and guided myself forward. I heard the swish of the automatic doors. I wanted to turn and yell, "D-a-d-d-y." Too late, the doors closed behind me.

I heard a voice. "I am with you," from deep inside me. *Was that real or…? That's not how God sounds. Is it? Terrific…now I was hallucinating.*

Panic. My knees knocked together. My heart raced like a long–distance runner. I leaned against a cool tile wall. Afraid I might fall, I considered praying. A nasal female voice from the dark asked, "May I help you?"

Surprisingly, I managed to form coherent words. "I can't see. I've lost my vision." The nasal voice grabbed my arm and guided me into a wheelchair. She placed my feet on the foot rests. "Do you have insurance? Give me your purse and I'll find your card." Cool air blew across my cheeks. The wheelchair and squishy shoe noises raced forward.

Timidly, I handed over my purse and held my spinning head. "I'm so dizzy again," I told the unseen person.

"Lean on me, and let's get you up here onto the gurney." She covered me with a blanket, and tucked the rough edges under my sides. "I'll get the doctor," her voice trailed off into the distance.

A few minutes later a baritone voice, said "Mrs. Oles, I'm Doctor Wayne. Are you here alone?"

"No, not now. You're here." His cold stethoscope moved on my chest.

"Mrs. Oles, can you describe me?" the baritone voice pulled on my eyelids.

"You're a dark blob."

"Am I wearing glasses?"

"I can't tell you what hair color you have, much less if you're wearing glasses."

A medical whirlwind began around me. Doctors and nurses tried to get me to read charts I couldn't see. Instruments that felt very odd checked my corneas, and blood work was ordered. CAT scans were ordered, and unfamiliar voices came at me from near and far. Tender hands and rough hands touched me and pulled me. Questions were asked and re–asked. It had only been a few hours, according to a nurse, but it felt like a lifetime.

You don't have to see people's facial expressions to hear concern in their voices.

"Kerrie," the baritone voice patted my shoulder. "Is there someone we can call? We're going to admit you."

I wanted to tell them my dad was probably on his fifth cigarette and circling the parking lot, but restrained myself, "No, not really." I tried to swallow the lump in my throat. Reality dawned. I was very much alone in the blurred darkness.

"We're not sure what is causing this," a calm voice in the black fog said. "You might be having a stroke or an aneurism."

What did he say? That happens to old people, not me!

Another deeper voice, "It could be a brain tumor. We just don't know at this time, but we'll run tests to pinpoint the problem."

"Is this dark blurredness going to go away? I asked.

The sharpest voice, a woman's, "They don't know if the blindness is temporary or not at this time. It's a wait-and-see status."

There it was…

Permanent blindness was to be my fate; I'd be lost in a sea of gray–black uncertainty forever. *Phillip, why are you in L.A.? I need you.*

Caleb and Cameron's sweet cherub faces flashed in my mind. Agony gripped my entire being. *Was this really happening? How could I live through this?* Now alone in the dismal antiseptic ER room, I was experiencing my worst fears.

Obsessed with how I would die from age eleven… this had to be my way…my time.

Another invisible chain wrapped around my body.

Not the first.

Lifeline

I lay in my hospital bed in solitary gray darkness. David Letterman signed off the TV for the night. Now the crackle static from the overhead television began to annoy me. Oh, how I wish a nurse would come into my room. If I was asleep, she'd find a reason to take my blood pressure or temperature, anything to disturb me. I groped for the remote. No luck. The bed growled its gears to adjust itself downward. Oops. Wrong button. My chin quivered. My teeth chattered. I coiled into a tighter ball and wished for another blanket. Periodic flashes of black and gray lights danced around me. The flashes teased my eyelids and brought comfort to me at the same time.

In the quietness of the gray–black flashes, a soft squeak from the door to my room startled me. Oh, how I hoped it was a nurse. A cleaning woman? Anyone, someone, hopefully that could get me a blanket.

The unforgettable smell of my husband's cologne filled the air. I felt Phillip's loving presence enter the room. His familiar footsteps approached my bed. One shoe dropped to the floor with a low thud, then the other. His warm breath soothed my ear. He whispered, "I love you." He crawled into the narrow bed and held me in his arms. He had flown all night on the red–eye to get home to me. No more words were spoken, they weren't needed. I absorbed his strength and cried myself to sleep. Finally, a man I could depend on.

My lifeline had arrived.

No eye has seen, no ear has heard, and no mind has conceived what God has prepared for those who love him. (NIV)

1 Corinthians 2:9

Chapter 3

THE TESTING POINT

Over the next two days, I was given medication of tablets, capsules, and liquid. I was poked with needles and probed by mysterious cold metal instruments. I was X-rayed from every position and angle imaginable and had countless CAT scans and blood tests. In between each test, doctors and nurses opened the door to my room. They asked the most irritating question, "Can you see Mrs. Oles?" Or "any improvement?"

"No," I answered every time. We had to eliminate everything to determine what was causing the blindness. Test after test, result after result, I didn't know whether to breathe a sigh of relief, or have a tantrum because the problem still existed. *What is wrong with me?*

Mom telephoned constantly, because I wouldn't allow her to bring the children to the hospital. She never asked why she couldn't bring the boys there, and for that I was grateful. I couldn't stand the thought that I couldn't see their faces.

Mom asked questions about the tests and sent Dad with more hand lotion or toothpaste, any excuse to be involved. Dad was kept busy running errands back and forth to the hospital.

They couldn't stand it because they weren't there to query the doctors, I guess a parent thing.

Each time Mom and I talked on the telephone, the conversation ended with her irritating statement. "You're fine. You're all right. Believe that in your heart and accept it." That was easy for her to say; she had eyesight. If that was faith, she had enough for both of us. Or was she in denial?

Friends from church called to pray for me, but from my faithless pit of fear, no one inspired a spark of hope. I was too focused on "poor pitiful me." Forever blind was my fate. I was convinced I'd never see my boys grow into men. Look into the pools of my husband's blue eyes, or see the waves crash against the seashore. An air of depression hung in the atmosphere of my room like a heavy, wet blanket.

A second MRI was scheduled on the third day for 8:00 A.M. The doctor explained they hadn't taken pictures of the base of my neck. They needed to explore the small arteries of my neck for an aneurism. I was devastated to face the large, clanking birth chamber again. My claustrophobia might kick in this time. The first test had been relatively short, but the new MRI test would take forty–five minutes, and would pinpoint the problem.

Little did I know…

Pinpoint the Problem

Bacon and sausage aromas filled the hallway. The noisy breakfast cart clattered to a stop outside my room. "Phil?"

He patted my hand, "I'm right here, honey. I'm starving. I think I'm going to run to the cafeteria for some breakfast. There's a nurse here to see you. I'll be here when you get back. I promise."

"Good morning, Mrs. Oles. I'll be taking you for your MRI test," a cheery voice said. "I'll let you ride on the gurney so you won't get dizzy. Scoot over onto it." She patted my left shoulder to show me the direction to move.

I wanted to bark at her, "I'd rather go to breakfast with my husband" or "Why do you sound so cheerful, lady? Don't you know I'm blind, and wearing a paper gown that gaps in the back?"

"How could God love such a person as me?"

Light and dark flashes teased my eyes. Vibrations of the gurney's wobbly wheels reminded me of my bumpy roads in life. Maybe it's true, your life really does flash before your eyes when you have a near-death experience. Past scenes of failures, hurts, arguments, and disappointments that I'd caused to myself and loved ones darted in and out of my mind. If my family knew all I had done in earlier years, they wouldn't like me, much less love me. How could God love such a person as me? This must be my punishment.

Why oh why, God? I'm a good person now. I deserved blindness or death many times years ago, but not now. Maybe I needed to remind Him I attend the largest church in the Dallas–Fort Worth area and have for eight years. I tried to be involved in all the "right" things of the church. I volunteered my help for different programs. Why, I visited nursing homes. I read to the elderly and brought them fresh flowers, hand–picked from my yard, and sweet lovely wrapped gifts, brightening their day; I'm a good person.

I began to bargain with God, a let's–make–a–deal type promise.

Why now, God? Hadn't I earned the right, like my friends, to watch my sons grow into young men?

Which awful sin had I done to cause this? Why have I always been different? Didn't I deserve some good stuff in my life? God needed to answer my questions and answer them now. Why oh why, me, God? I wondered if anyone else had felt this way.

Splashes of a heavy wet mop. The stench of Pine Sol turned my empty stomach. An alto female voice hummed "Amazing, grace, how sweet the sound." Her notes seemed to vibrate low in her throat, heavy like the wet mop I knew she was using. A lump developed deep in my throat. I couldn't swallow. The hymn haunted me.

"Amazing Grace"- where is it? And what do the words really mean?

"Here we are again," the cheery voice stated. "You remember Mrs. Oles from the other day, don't you Roberta? We'll help you onto the MRI table." I heard a pat on a hard surface.

Roberta, the MRI nurse, instructed, "You can listen to the radio through the headset, but I suggest you keep your eyes closed and try to relax. If you move, we'll have to do the pictures over, and I know you don't want to repeat for the third time. Try to relax."

"The hymn haunted me."

Did she say relax? Surely she was joking. Maybe I needed to fill her in on the horror movie inside my head. If I hadn't heard the old song, I might not have been as nice.

Reminders of sins, both past and present, filled my irregular heartbeats. *Okay, God, I deserve to be blind, I conceded, but please let me live. Don't let me have anything wrong with my brain.* I had lived my entire life one step away from Jesus. He seemed to be at arm's length from my tormented soul. Hidden.

Scared and nervous, the only thing I could think to do was pray. Nothing else had helped.

Should I beg?

How should I start?

Is prayer your steering wheel or your spare tire?

Corrie Ten Boom

Chapter 4

THE 23rd PSALM

The 23rd Psalm popped into my throbbing head. Maybe I'll pass the time by saying that prayer.

"Here are your headphones. You can listen to music during the test," Roberta said handing me the outer space apparatus.

Great. I hope they can block out the bad scenes running in my head, I thought sliding them onto my ears. The whirl of the huge MRI machine started up.

My prayer and thoughts merged. I inched forward into what felt like a birth canal.

> *The Lord is my shepherd; I shall not want. He makes me to lie down in green pastures; He leads me beside the still waters. He restores my soul; He leads me in the paths of righteousness for His name's sake. Yea, though I walk through the valley of the shadow of death, I will fear no evil; for You are with me; Your rod and Your staff, they comfort me; You prepare a table before me in the presence of my enemies; You anoint my head with oil; my cup runs over. Surely goodness and mercy shall follow me all the days of my life; and I will dwell in the house of the Lord forever.*

What had made me think of the 23rd Psalm? Was it the mournful, low voice humming "Amazing Grace"? Is it because scenes in the movies show people reciting the Psalm right before, or after someone dies? The clanks vibrated around me. I refuse to think about the annoying clank noises; I'll think about the Psalm.

The Lord is my shepherd...

The words have never made much sense to me. Why does the prayer refer to him as a shepherd? Are we a flock of sheep?

I shall not want...

Ha, that's a joke – seems I've wanted many things that I didn't get. Lots of things I don't have and probably never will. I guess I haven't done without necessities, but I sure have wanted more luxuries. What I'd give to be rich and famous. I'm cheap – I'd settle for a new house or car. Paying bills on time would be nice also.

And, *He makes me to lie down in green pastures* – What's that about?

Lord, I appreciate lovely green fields, but I'm not in the habit of going to a local field and lying down. This area doesn't have many green fields, and if there are any, they have cattle or horses. There are zillions of cars, concrete, noise, and millions of people, but green fields? Rarely. Nor, do I want to lie down in one.

He leads me beside the still waters? I squeezed my eyes tighter to visualize a calm lake scene. What help is that, God? I love the water; I feel alive immersed in water. I love swimming pools, lakes, and especially the ocean. Maybe that's what He meant.

He restores my soul…I don't need my soul restored. I need my eyes restored!

I became indignant. Maybe this prayer isn't for me, just another example of my failures. Holy cow. I can't even pray right. Is there a right or wrong way to pray?

He leads me in the paths of righteousness…

I don't need my soul restored. I need my eyes restored!

Righteousness? That almost made me laugh out loud. I missed that path. I know for a fact I have never gone down the path of righteousness. I'm stumped.

"Now lie still. Don't move." Roberta's voice echoed inside the tube.

The fear of all the bad possibilities inside my body made me balk at praying the next line.

Yea, though I walk through the valley of the shadow of death, I will fear no evil:

Death…. I couldn't think on that memory now – not yet.

These three days were the shadow of death.

I will fear no evil…

Are you kidding me? The evil one has had my address all along. He has enticed, captured, and had me bound for as long as I can remember. I knew the devil, is the one who kills, steals, and destroys. I'd learned that much from attending church, that and I had memorized the 23rd Psalm.

For you are with me…

Tears filled my eyes, and then I realized. I had pinpointed problems that had nothing to do with my arteries.

The realization finally came.

I didn't believe God had been with me my entire life. If He had been watching over me, why had all the bad things happened? The God of the universe could not love me. Who am I?

I believe they call the Psalm the promise prayer. If that's so, as I scan the pages of my mind, why haven't any of these promises come true?

I will fear no evil…

Is this ever going to end?

Frozen frames of my past became ever present in my mind. The temperature seemed to drop twenty degrees inside the MRI tube. The chill that penetrated my body threw me back to that chilling night in 1972 when I certainly did fear evil.

Chilling FEAR

I was four–years-old. Mom and I had said my now-I-lay-me prayers. She tucked me into my Raggedy Ann canopy bed, tenderly kissed me goodnight, and softly closed my bedroom door. I snuggled under the warm bunny rabbit sheets that smelled of lemon fabric softener.

As I dozed off to sleep, I pushed Tina, my life-size doll, out of bed. I reached to pick her up and heard the front door slam. Angry voices came from the living room. Was it one of my brothers? Of course, I wasn't supposed to get out of bed, but being a nosy little sister and idolizing my three brothers, I snuck down the hallway to see what was happening. I hid in the narrow corner beside Mom's upright piano.

The corner between Mom's piano and the living room wall was my haven. She'd play beautiful music while I curled up in the corner and listened. Her fingers danced up and down the keyboard. Sometimes I'd dance, pretending I was a ballerina, when she played a waltz called the *Blue Danube*. She knew I was there, but the music absorbed us, both lost in our own melodies of life. Mom couldn't carry a tune in a hatbox, but she made the white and black keys come alive to your ears, toes, and soul.

This night there was no music in the corner – just evil itself, and the evil one was my middle brother, Joe Ray.

He was the brother who always had time for me. He played dolls with me when the other two brothers weren't around. Of course, he was the Ken doll and I was the fairy princess, Barbie.

Most of all we played games. Operation was our favorite. We spent hours removing the tiny parts and laughing. No matter who won or lost, tickling was always the biggest part of our fun.

Why was Joe Ray standing in the middle of the living room screaming? I had to cover my ears to block out his cruel words.

"Where is he? I'm going to kill Clint! I'm going to kill him!" Joe Ray screamed with clinched fists, head tossed back, and legs crouched like a wild animal ready to pounce.

Mom and Dad were watching TV. Dad leaped from his chair and grabbed Joe Ray from behind in a bear hug. Joe Ray's arms and legs kicked and twisted like a possessed string–puppet. He wrenched away from

Dad's grip. Instantly, Joe Ray spun around and for a split second, his wicked eyes pierced into mine. Killer eyes of stone hatred. I huddled in the corner, paralyzed in terror.

I heard the voice of the devil himself. "C-l-i-n-t," Joe Ray screamed once more, "I'm going to kill you. You hear me? Where are you?" He yelled into the air; his neck muscles bulged. He twisted his head back and forth trying to get free from Dad's grip, legs kicking into the air.

Clint came around the corner from the kitchen. Joe Ray slipped from Dad's grip and charged at Clint. Dad grabbed him around his waist once again. Mom screamed and cried at the same time, her face white with horror.

"Go to your room and lock the door," Daddy yelled to Clint. Clint ran down the hall to his room.

Then my daddy, my protector, lifted Joe Ray into the air and threw him to the floor. Dad gasped for breath from the struggle, "Help me hold him, oh, God, help me hold him," he pleaded to Mom. They pinned Joe Ray there for a long time. Joe Ray twisted, screamed, and moaned with every possible vile motion. Terror flooded my corner haven like rushing water from a broken dam.

My protector and my tickle games were washed away, lost forever in a single act of evil. If only I hadn't gotten out of bed.

I never stood by the piano again, and Mom sold it soon after that night of horror.

I formed my view of my earthly father, and ultimately my view of my heavenly Father from a night of evil.

I could never tell anyone what I had seen.

A father that could punish me if ever I misbehaved badly and a father I was afraid to disappoint. The similarity between my earthly father and my heavenly Father was formed by a scene I should not have witnessed.

While my parents weren't looking, I slipped back to my room, unnoticed and hid under the covers with my doll Tina, shivered, and cried until I fell asleep. Innocence watched as my brother became a scary monster, capable of terrible things. I could never tell anyone what I had seen, not even Mom.

Why did Joe Ray want to kill Clint?

I was too young to know about drugs and a bad LSD trip. My parents were unfamiliar with such things as well, but they met them face-to-face in our living room. That night, everyone survived, but the musical magic between Mom's piano and my corner died.

Fear no evil. What a ridiculous statement for a prayer. I saw chilling fear of evil that night beside the piano. The first link in the invisible chain that bound my heart was shackled to my innocent four-year-old body. Wounds were created that lasted a life time and fear settled in my heart. It made its home so profoundly deep that I would struggle with fear my entire life. How can I be anything but fearful? My insides screamed silently, I could be blind or worse than that, this could lead to my death.

Ugh...Death.

That was definitely not what I wanted to remember now. Not that memory. I must be near death. Why else would this horror movie be playing inside my head?

"You're doing great, Mrs. Oles. Remember, no moving. Try to lie perfectly still," the MRI nurse chided me.

How do you lie still while facing death?

Therefore, if anyone is in Christ, he is a new creation; the old has gone, the new has come!(NIV)

2 Corinthians 5:17

Chapter 5

THE "D" WORD

Let's see – where was I? I'll start over, can't hurt. I have plenty of time.

The Lord is my shepherd; I shall not want. He makes me to lie down in green pastures. He leads me beside the still waters. He restores my soul; He leads me in the paths of righteousness for His name's sake. Yea, though I walk through the valley of the shadow of death.

There it is: the "D" word.

I can't finish the prayer; just to think of the word death hurts my brain. It's like someone's nails scratching a blackboard.

God, when did you stop loving me? I wondered as I lay inside the MRI tube. Was it on December 26, 1979?

The memories still hurt. . .

"Kerrie, time to get up," Grandpa called. He sounded different, anxious, and his voice was harsh. Normally he woke me by tickling a feather under my nose or on my cheek and that always made me giggle. The days and nights at my grandparents' home were the most precious memories in my eleven years, but today everything was wrong.

This day there was no feather; there was no giggle. In fact, the house was deadly– eerie quiet. I got out of bed, put on my new pink fuzzy robe and matching slippers, and scuffed into the kitchen. Cold toast and a glass of milk set on the kitchen table. Grandpa always made me French toast with maple syrup powdered sugar sprinkled on top, and always chocolate milk. Something was very wrong.

Yesterday had been a wonderful Christmas day. Mom and Dad had bought me the doll I wanted with her matching convertible car, Grandma and Grandpa gave me some cool clothes, and the family had eaten lots of turkey and Grandma’s famous pumpkin pie.

Was I in trouble? What could I have done while I slept? I mulled over the list of no–no’s at my grandparents’ house. The list was short, because I could do no wrong in their eyes. What had happened?

Grandpa said he needed to talk to me. My fear accelerated. Then he said the words that forever changed my life. “Clint is gone. He isn’t coming back.”

Maybe I was still sleepy, but I couldn’t understand. Clint, my oldest brother was gone.

Yesterday I had helped him carry in his Christmas gifts from his brand new yellow Thunderbird. The car was big and beautiful, and smelled so new and fresh, but I liked his old car, the red and white GTO Pontiac, better. On the weekends, we washed his car together. Sometimes he sprayed me with the water hose and I pretended to be mad. He rubbed the soap on the car and I dried the shiny silver wheel covers. Clint was cool. His long blonde hair blew in the wind. The sunshine bounced off his peace necklace; flashes of silver lights shined in my face. Flashy, unbuttoned silk shirts, bell bottom jeans, clunky wedge shoes, and his beautiful white, toothy smile were my fondest memories of my oldest brother. He was voted class favorite, and was so popular he seemed like a movie star.

My grandpa attempted to explain.

Clint, was not coming back. To this day, those are the only words from that morning I can recall Grandpa saying. Not coming back. After all, I had hugged Clint last night under the mistletoe. He smelled heavenly. His cologne still tickled my nostrils and made me smile. The beautiful gift wrapping from the perfume bottle he gave me yesterday was on the dresser. What did that mean, he wasn't coming back? I didn't know Clint had left, except to go to his apartment.

Had Clint died?

Late Christmas night, my parents had driven back home to Oklahoma. While I sat in shock at the kitchen table, they arrived from Tulsa. Kenny, my 6'2", 250-pound, youngest brother, arrived next with his shotgun. He wanted to kill the drunk driver who had passed out behind the wheel of his pickup truck, crossed four lanes of expressway, and killed our brother. I heard the commotion and ran outside to watch Dad and Grandpa wrestle Kenny to take away his shotgun.

An adult movie unfolded–one I was too young to view or understand. It seemed the family was always coping with Joe Ray's drug–related problems. Now Kenny, the black–haired, blue–eyed, All–American, football hero had burst into the scene with a shotgun. This couldn't be happening. Pain piled in on me faster than I could absorb it.

For the next few days, I felt invisible, shuffled here and there, back and forth, because I was too young to be included in the movie. Mom and Dad thought they were protecting me, but I stood among strangers and relatives alone, isolated.

My fear of *being alone* was born.

At the graveside funeral, my grandparents' pastor said something about God. God. I wondered where he might be. Was he really there? God was far away in a place called heaven, at least that's what the pastor had said the few times I attended my grandparents' church. He was the one who would punish me if I disappointed him, the mean, powerful one. Right?

As the pastor spoke at the closed casket, graveside service, I stared at the picture of my brother's smiling face from on top of his casket and wondered, *What does Clint look like inside the big pretty box?*

The razor wind cut my wet cheeks and I couldn't feel my frozen toes. The chill factor was minus five degrees, I heard someone say. Kenny reached for my hand, his bitter cold fingers wrapped around my hand. I remember thinking, *Maybe they want me to be the one gone, and not Clint.* Life as I knew it was definitely about to change. Forever.

I sat in the cold metal chair between my brother Kenny and my parents, trying to smile at the people who passed by. They spoke kind words to me, but I was distracted. Where was my brother, Joe Ray? My focus was drawn away from the casket to a black and white police car that stopped by the curb near the service. Joe Ray stepped from the backseat dressed in Clint's pin-striped suit. No one had prepared me for the scene that unfolded. Everyone turned to look at him. He gathered more attention than my deceased brother. I didn't know that Joe Ray had been arrested the day before for drugs and parole violation. My dad had thrown himself on the mercy of the courts, begging for Joe Ray not to be transported to prison until after the funeral. Since Dad

"No one prepared me for the scene that unfolded."

had coached football with the two arresting officers, they agreed to be responsible for the prisoner. They were willing to escort him to the funeral, but they failed to mention he would be in jailhouse chains.

Grief and shock overtook me, seeing Joe Ray in Clint's pin-striped suit, bound in chains that hung from his wrists, waist, and ankles. Why was he in chains? I was confused. Policemen are good people. They arrest criminals, protect, and serve, but they had brought my brother to the funeral bound in chains. How could they? Joe Ray was the kind brother, the one who always took care of me, played games with me, and fixed my broken toys. Nothing made sense to me. Clint was dead, and Joe Ray was at the funeral in chains.

The events of Christmas 1979 totally undid me. It was as though someone pushed me in a closet and said, "Okay, now put your grown-up dress on and live with it." I was locked away waiting for the "one" who would unlock and comfort my pain. I would continue to look for that someone for many years.

The chains that bound my brother clanked in the frozen air, echoing off the headstones throughout the cemetery. I can still hear those haunting noises. With each clank, our hearts broke. My own emotional chains rattled when I walked away from the gravesite. Though the chains were invisible, they shackled my young body. No one was there to unlock them. The image of Joe Ray in Clint's pin–striped suit, bound in chains, is still frozen in my memory.

The MRI tube banged, and sputtered with its loud sounds as the test continued. Even in my health crisis, all I heard was chains echoing off headstones.

That day, I began to hate the "D" word and still do.

The Hero

The Pastor took one look at my family and knew we needed a hero. Clint, as the oldest sibling, had been the "hero" to my two brothers and me. Too soon he was taken from our lives. The pastor who presided over Clint's funeral introduced me to Jesus Christ on December 28, 1979. In a side room at the funeral home, he told me the story of salvation. The hero he talked about didn't fly out of the sky wearing a red cape. I only had to believe in Jesus and quietly ask Him to live in my heart. His red cape was the blood He shed for my sins on the cross of Calvary. Too young to grasp the full salvation story, I stayed at arm's length away from Him.

Distant.

Yet another "D" word, another link in the chains of my past.

Clank. Clank. Lying here I wonder, *Is this my "D" word day?*

Was I distant for too long and now my fate is death? As the movie reels of my life keep rolling, I reflect back on many things left unsaid, time that was wasted, and above all, the many unanswered questions.

Man appears for a little while to laugh and weep, to work and play, and then to go to make room for those who shall follow him in the never-ending cycle.

Aiden Wilson Tozner

Chapter 6

THE UNANSWERED QUESTION

Did everyone think I would forget Clint? That his memories would fade into blankness? The unanswered question– what did Clint look like inside the unopened box? They say that time heals, but the exact opposite is true for me. Over and over, I recall things that they thought I would never remember.

Even small details like the pin–striped suit take me back to happier days.

Thirsty because I had played Hide and Seek all morning with the neighborhood children, I ran into the house for a quick drink of water. Clint and my parents were sitting at the kitchen table talking and drinking coffee.

"Yeah, with my promotion and raise, I can buy a new car. I'm thinking about a Corvette or a Thunderbird," Clint boasted with a wide, crooked grin. "Hi, little sis," he winked and waved at me.

"Well, with this windfall you have to buy a pin-striped suit, blue of course, to match your eyes," Mom said, "because if you have a high-paying job, *and* a new car, a pin-striped suit is a must. It says to the world *I have arrived, I'm successful.*" Everyone laughed when Mom placed her thumbs under her armpits and stuck out her chest.

I gulped a couple of swallows of orange juice to wash down the chocolate chip cookie. Not knowing what a pin-striped suit was, I envisioned a suit with ballpoint pens all over it. *How ugly would that be, and why would he want that?*

Still, to this day, I think of him whenever I see a man in a blue pin-striped suit. However, there was an occasion twelve years after the "D" word that I've tried desperately to block out.

Long years later on Friday, payday, I stood in line at my bank, waiting for the next available teller. The line zigzagged along a maze of ropes. The next customer, a distinguished older man stepped to the teller's window. He, obviously a C.E.O., and the teller were balancing the federal deficit since he was taking so long. I drummed my fingers on my purse. Then I stopped cold. He wore a blue pin–striped suit. The gentleman was taller than my brother Clint, but had the same hair color. Memories of Clint flooded my mind: Car washes, a peace necklace that reflected the sunshine, and clunky wedge shoes brought a smile to my face.

Odd– after so many years gone by– no tears came, one of the few times the memory didn't hurt. The pin–striped suit made me grin. Then, out of nowhere, my warm memories shattered.

"Hello there," a stranger said to me. "Aren't you Clint's little sister, Kerrie? I'm Kim. I use to date Clint back in high school."

Jerked back to reality, I thought how ironic it was to see her when I was thinking about him.

"Oh, yes, I remember you," I lied and returned her hug.

"How are you doing?" she asked. "I haven't seen you in a long time, since the funeral to be exact. I felt badly for you and your family. Especially knowing Clint had been decapitated."

Did she just say decapitated? Did she think I knew that disturbing detail? I had *no* idea. Did I need to hear that bit of information in the teller line at the bank?

December, 1979, returned, immediately jabbing me in the stomach. My legs weakened; my mind remembered the portrait on the casket. My question answered, twelve years later. . . *Now I knew what Clint looked like inside the big, pretty box. Why had I ever asked the question?*

Was Joe Ray trying to fill Clint's shoes by wearing the pin-striped suit at his funeral that day? The suit couldn't hide the chains around his wrists, waist, and ankles. Joe Ray's invisible chains still have him bound. He has long been released from prison, several times, but he serves a life-sentence to drugs and alcohol.

I remain thankful that on that fateful Christmas Day, Clint gave each family member an 8x10 portrait of himself in his blue shirt, tie, and pin-striped suit. His eyes sparkle from the portrait, and his crooked smile will forever say, "Hi, little sis." (Wonder if Clint smiled down from heaven when he saw the picture on his own casket?)

Decapitation!

Another "D" word.

I want off the "D" words. I can't think on such depressing memories any longer.

I want this movie to stop playing inside my head. Okay- where was I in the prayer?

For You are with me;

I don't feel you with me. There are numerous unanswered questions in life; and now the frustration of blindness. Maybe the prayer isn't for me after all.

The replay of my life is like being in the eye of a tornado. Clanks and swirls all around me, just like in this tube. The music in my ear isn't drowning out the scenes in my head.

Your rod and Your staff, they comfort me...

Rod? And Staff? I have no idea what that means. Comfort. I recall the day I found comfort during a tornado. I feel like these days of testing have been a tornado. It makes me wonder, *Who was really with me that fateful day?*

The Tornado

I scrambled down the hill. Safety. That was all I could think. I lunged for the gate to our farm. *I must reach the house as fast as I can*. The tornado siren blared in the distance; its shrieks blended into the heavy dark cloud above me. I struggled to shut the front door, wind so strong I had to use all my strength. With shaking hands, I was barely able to dial the telephone.

"Mom, come home quick. It's a tornado. What'll I do?"

"Stay calm, Honey," Mom soothed. "I'll be there as quick as I can, but it's raining so hard here I can't even see my car, much less get to it. I'll leave work as soon as I can. Take the mattress or covers off of your bed and get in the far corner of your closet. Put them over you and pray."

"Please, come home with me." I cried. Even though I was thirteen, I needed my mom. "I'm scared. Please."

"I know, baby. I'll be there. I promise."

I slammed down the phone and ran to my room. I yanked the covers off the bed and huddled inside the crowded closet. Shoes and dirty clothes surrounded me. The walls sucked in and out with the rhythmic gushes of wind. It sounded as if a freight train was outside our house.

Mom why aren't you here? You know I hate to be alone!

My science teacher's voice echoed in my head. "If you're ever in a tornado, get between or under rocks or a ditch. The rocks can shelter you from objects that can be flying at high rates of speed."

Determined not to be alone in the house, I grabbed the bundle of covers, and sprinted out my front door. The wind roared. Treetops bent to touch the ground. I had to reach the ditch in the front of our property. Two huge rocks stood like solid mountains, I figured if the rocks couldn't be moved by my dad's bulldozer; that would be the safest place to hide.

"Timidly, I emerged from the rocks."

I wedged myself between the rock–mountains and slid my body underneath to safety, with covers overhead. Thoughts ran in and out of my mind as I listened to the storm blow over. Then as suddenly as it blew in; it stopped.

Comfort. Shielded from the rain. Calm wind.

By the time mom arrived at the farm, all was serene. Only a slight mist fell. I heard the car roar to a stop. "Kerrie," her panicked voice hung on the wet mist. "Where are you?"

Timidly, I emerged from the rocks. "Are you okay? I came as quick as I could," she patted my cheek. "I saw the damage in the neighborhood. Trees are down and every house has broken windows. How wise of you to think about the rocks, God showed you where to seek safety."

"I'm okay, I guess, but look at the house!"

We both looked up at the roof damage on the outside of the house. A large tree limb now occupied my closet. Mom and I held each other and cried.
For You are with me; Your rod and Your staff, they comfort me.

Tears fell from my eyes. I realized that the rocks weren't the only things that covered me that day. *Where are you now, God?*

Okay, Kerrie...

Calm yourself and lie still. I can feel every organ crying out, desperate for you, God to be with me <u>*now*</u>*. I began to repeat myself, even in silence.*

The Lord is my shepherd; I shall not want. He makes me to lie down in green pastures; He leads me beside the still waters. He restores my soul; He leads me in the paths of righteousness for His name's sake. Yea, though I walk through the valley of the shadow of death, I will fear no evil; for You are with me; Your rod and Your staff, they comfort me. You prepare a table before me in the presence of my enemies; You anoint my head with oil; my cup runs over. Surely goodness and mercy shall follow me all the days of my life; and I will dwell in the house of the Lord forever.

Your rod and Your staff, they comfort me...

I wish I understood the prayer. A *rod* – is that going to prod me along in life? If the rod is to guide me in the right direction, why have I missed all the right turns? Mine were all left turns. Maybe my navigation system was on the blink. Do I have my dad's genes, the kind that won't stop to ask directions?

A *staff* - isn't that like a cane? I think you use a staff to steady your walk. Maybe you use the staff as a pointer, like turn signals in a car? Either way – I don't feel much comfort, especially inside this tube.

Life's a puzzle and I'm missing a piece. I think I have lots of missing pieces and the doctors can't complete the puzzle either. Hobby shops have glue to pour over a completed puzzle before framing it to hang on the wall. Let me see– glue, frame, nail, maybe those are my missing pieces. Could a carpenter fix me?

Wasn't Jesus a carpenter?

Do others feel they have missing pieces, like me? Am I the only one to feel this way? I think my mind is rambling. The clanks are driving me crazy.

"You're wiggling, Mrs. Oles," Roberta's nagging voice echoed again.

If X-rays could capture your mind's images, she would have known why tears trailed down my face making it even harder not to move.

Please be almost finished.

I'm almost at the end of my chain– did I think chain? I mean rope.

Does blindness make you think about your shadowy past? So desperate to seek light that you search the corners of your soul to recall the most regrettable things you've done?

Mistakes and sins you have blocked and never talked about with anyone. Does everyone have rattle–bone skeletons in the closet, hiding shocking secrets? I have them in my life. The sins you think God could never forgive you for.

What's the next line in the prayer?

You prepare a table before me in the presence of my enemies...

That's it. *That* is the sin I believe God can't forgive.

Ugh. The last thing I want to think about is all the men in my life.

Especially "him."

Glad I didn't think of him at the beginning. Forty-five minutes is an eternity to relive horrendous, unpleasant memories.

His memories puncture my brain like an ice-pick. Why? The enemy abuses.

For I am convinced that neither death nor life, neither angels nor demons, neither the present nor the future, nor any powers, neither height nor depth, nor anything else in all creation, will be able to separate us from the love of God that is in Christ Jesus our Lord.(NIV)

Romans 8:38

Chapter 7

THE ABUSER

I feel abused inside this tube. Is the ill treatment ever going to end?

I buried my enemy memories deep in the backyard of my mind, and never wanted to dig him up again. Now as low as I feel, our turbulent relationship comes to the forefront of this atrocious movie that's playing inside my head. I never wanted to think about my abuser again.

Never …

"You need any sauce?" The girl behind the counter asked. "Regular or spicy?"

"Oh, spicy of course," I grabbed three packets of spicy salsa, the burrito bag, and streaked to my car; my taste buds watering in anticipation.

On my way home, I drove down a deserted side street, a song from my first wedding blared from the radio. I barely remember being eighteen; it seems like forever ago. I still have the worn–out yellow towels from the wedding shower– just not the husband. Boy, what a kid I was, naïve and stupid. Too afraid to go to either of the colleges that gave me scholarships, or to be on my own, I joined wedded bliss with the class clown who said he loved me. He did for six months, but our marriage was the joke. I gave up an education. He gave up nothing, including dating.

I pressed the accelerator to exceed the speed limit– didn't want the burrito to get cold–and popped a disc into the CD player, hoping the nostalgic mood might pass me by.

No, luck. It didn't.

My mind ambled back to my second marriage. Within a few months of my divorce, I found a muscle–

bound body builder that I thought might be my rescuer. He loved me for five years, a record stretch in my life. Then I was single again – and alone. After two divorces before the age of twenty–six, dating was the last thing on my mind.

The car remote honked the horn to tell me I locked the car. I let the front door slam, tossed my keys onto the entry table, and flipped on the TV to the movie channel. *Pretty Woman.* “Perfect, I said to the television. “I’ve only watched this five times. I crossed my legs Indian style and adjusted the pillow behind me.

Oh, if life could be that, a fairytale come true.

Oh, if life could be that, a fairytale come true. I thought as I wiped a bit of cheese from my lip. A $1.25 burrito, new purple nail polish, and a chick flick. What a fun–filled Friday night. Oh well, it beats peanut butter on a stale bagel and expired milk. My cabinets and refrigerator were both so empty you could see the backside of the walls, almost as empty as my stomach. The next day was pay day, and I could remedy both situations. Wow! How sad, excited about making a grocery list. What a party animal I was. Tomorrow - look out Walmart, here I come.

What was that?

Thunder?

Someone was banging on my door. "All right, I'm coming," I tiptoed to look out the peephole. It was Gary, an acquaintance I had met a few weeks earlier at work.

"Yes?" I said through a half–opened door.

"Don't ever open the door without asking who it is. I could've been a rapist or meant you harm!"

His scolding reply made me think–*This person really cares about me.*

"What in the world are you doing here?" I opened the door wider.

"I saw your car at the taco place and thought you might need some real food. Cheap burritos will fill you up, but they aren't exactly a well-balanced meal," he smiled. A sack of Granola bars dropped from his hand.

"You brought me groceries? How nice of you," I was shocked.

"Where's the kitchen?" He flashed an appealing grin.

Not bad for an older man, I thought.

"This way, kind sir," I bowed at the waist. We laughed and made a game of putting the groceries away.

"My kitchen hasn't ever been this full. Looks like Walmart Super Center aisles inside my cabinets." I turned the oven to 425 degrees to cook the pot pies, and he found a knife to chop the lettuce for the salad.

Funny, it never occurred to me to ask how he knew where I lived. I was too grateful for the food.

We ate, laughed and talked for hours. A friendship started immediately. Gary impressed me with his knowledge and mature sophistication. He even had a little gray in his hair. I thought he was very distinguished looking. We gossiped about work, people at work, and who might be a couple, including some of our bosses. He described my routine shopping habits. He knew some of my friends, where they lived, and he admitted he'd observed me from afar. He commented that he hated my big zebra purse, but loved my black and white suit. The biggest surprise that he mentioned was being present at a karaoke contest, where I competed. He thought I looked great that night when I sang Patsy Cline's song "*Crazy*," and he was delighted I won the fifty dollar prize money. Most of all, he was quite taken with the unique sound of my voice. I realized he had watched me for some time, flattered in a way, I guess. My internal alarm did not go off, strictly because I was sidetracked about our mutual love in life. The thing I loved most in this world, the obsession that kept me sane, was the same pleasure he enjoyed most– music.

"Name a topic or title, and I can compose words in a few minutes," he bragged.

"All right, how about the topic rocky road," I suggested. To my amazement, he composed two verses and the chorus.

"I dreamed I'd be a Mariah Carey or Amy Grant music star."

I dreamed I'd be a Mariah Carey or Amy Grant music star. Gary saw himself as a Stevie Wonder or Clive Davis, a famous song–writer and producer. So the foundation was established. We agreed to make a demo CD and mail the CD to all the Nashville record companies. With my talent and his ability, there were no bounds to what we could accomplish. We'd become a team like June and Johnny Cash, or Ike and Tina Turner.

Determined to never give my heart away again, and desperate for new excitement, I jumped at anything that resembled the fix for this broken person, to fill my void. Gary, an older gentleman, might fill the vacant place of great loneliness within me. Friends with a mutual interest–that's all we could ever be, especially since he was ten years older than I, definitely a safe companion.

Looking back, it seems, after the "Death" word happened, all I ever did at home was stand in front of the full–length mirror in my room, holding my curling iron for the microphone in one hand, and pretend I was a famous singer. I can still hear Mom's annoying words interrupt me while I sang. "Kerrie, have you finished your homework. Quit singing and get your homework done."

She didn't understand that music helped me hide my pain from both her and dad. They cried for their sons in secret in their rooms. I sang to hide my pain. The spiritual songs made me feel alive. It didn't matter that I never understood the true meanings of the words.

Now, with this new friendship, all the practice might pay off.

When Gary and I weren't at work, we were busy writing lyrics and music for the demo CD. His encouragement made me believe dreams could and would come true. Driven by the search for success and elaborate dreams, I was lured and enticed into a false sense of reality. If I could become a famous personality, I could escape being who I was–someone I didn't care for.

I was washed overboard into a sea of fantasy.
My hook was baited.

Unaware I was the bait and the fish.

Lured and enticed by the thought of what we could be.

Enticement began.

The Enticement

One evening at Gary's apartment, he sat at the keyboard composing a chorus. "Christian music is the in thing right now to sing. The ready market," he said and struck a C–chord. "That'll be the genre for your voice. It's cutting edge, and I can write those words blindfolded."

He knew what was best for us, and I liked the music. Sounded good to me, and Lord knows I was ready– I could taste our sweet success.

My future looked star-studded. Dreams dangled in the front of my mind like shiny stars that lit up the night and my imagination. If I sang for God, He might allow me to make it big in the music industry just because I included Him. However, I was concerned that my personal life was too flawed. Perhaps this could change the way the Holy One viewed me. Especially after all the wrongs I'd committed. If I sang Christian music, God might love me. I had said the prayer of salvation when I was eleven. The only Holy One I knew was named Jesus Christ. Gary knew Him by other names.

"Jesus is merely a prophet. He shouldn't be your hero. You can sing about him and acquire success. Don't believe all the other stuff–just sing the songs on key," Gary grumbled. . . Slowly, I started to agree with him. After all, his argument sounded believable, and all the things he had me read discredited everything I had known. I heard his opinion so often that I began to agree. I adopted his belief because I didn't have a full understanding of my own.

As time passed, I began to realize Gary might be a stumbling block in my life, one that compared to a fatal attraction. I didn't see the crisis coming, but I certainly felt his impact. Tempted with desires of this world, I trusted and felt comfortable with the persuading that was whispered in my ear. Our music and our friendship were my only commitments, up to my chin with plans of fame and fortune via his convictions.

One evening when Gary was out of town, I longed for a girls' night out, a burger and a movie. Six telephone calls later–five rejections and one no answer–I realized communication with friends had faded. My world and time were occupied by Gary 24/7, especially since he didn't approve of any of my friends. He found fault with each and every friend. With no one else in my life, we grew deeper and stronger in our relationship, another horrendous decision on my part. We crossed the line from friendship to romance.

During studio time one evening, at a hundred dollars an hour, Gary became irate with me. From the control room, he hit the buzzer.

"Stop, stop, stop! What are you doing? Are you even thinking about this? I can't believe the money your parents are spending on you, and you're acting like your mind is in another hemisphere. Get your act together," he screamed over the speaker.

"I'm trying, but the note is odd. I can't hit it correctly," I complained.

"Try it again. This time, do it right" he ordered. "Can't you lower the song a key or two. Maybe then it would sound better."

"That's just the way you are. Me, me, me. That's all you think about. Yourself. It doesn't matter how many hours I spent on my music. Let's just please Kerrie," he whined to make fun of me. "Now try it again from the top."

"It rained white paper for thirty seconds."

The music began, and I dreaded for the chorus to start. I tried to hit the note. Flat, one more time.

The buzzer jarred me.

"Stop!" Gary charged into the studio room. He threw the sheet music everywhere. It rained white paper for thirty seconds. His nose to mine, "Listen to me," he shouted in my face. "You dumb country bumpkin. You're off key! Try it again. Get it right, or get out of here!" he screamed.

That night I walked home from the studio. The drizzling rain matted my hair to my head. Hairspray and mascara ran into my eyes. I know I looked like a homeless person with no comb or personal hygiene. Damp clothes clung to my body. With each soggy step, I became angrier with myself. Oddly, I wasn't mad at Gary; I was ashamed of myself. Why couldn't I get anything right? Gary's word games had finally taken its toll on my already wounded ego. I plummeted through the never ending hole of despair; I searched for the bottom – anything to stop my descent. Where I finally landed, was too far down to climb out – too hopeless to care. The once cordial and caring man changed his melodies to physical and verbal abuse. The evil one was trying to fill me up with a slow drip of his lies.

The list of *who* Kerrie was – was a very long list. In case I had forgotten, he would remind me daily of the living, breathing picture of failure before his eyes. Words like *stupid, disappointment, worthless, and burden* were regular comments he aimed at me.

If we played the flip side of my CD, our songs of love played backward. Unraveling. I became a wad of gum stuck to the bottom of Gary's shoe. Only a nuisance.

Gary began to drain my existence from my very being.

A master of disguises–he was happy one minute and on a tear the next. Still, I was all he had to work with. He had to make do with the talent we both brought to the table, and he hated that – or me?

Days dragged into weeks, and weeks into months after we mailed the CD's. We awaited our big break phone call. With only a few responses to our dream lifeline, Gary realized that this simple country girl had not done her part. Fame and fortune eluded us.

There was no escape. I was caged like a helpless animal. I had chosen him, I had chosen this Hell. I needed someone to rescue me.

Captured, confused, and scared I did nothing.

You might as well try to hear without ears or breathe without lungs, as to try to live a Christian life without the Spirit of God in your heart.

D.L. Moody

Chapter 8

THE CAPTIVE

I was a captive in Gary's world, his sole possession. Isolated. Alone.

I hated to be ALONE.

Total capture began the day fight left my body.

Gary telephoned to suggest that I wear my black and white suit he loved for our date. I wanted to wear my new brown sundress, but he insisted. It was a good hair day, make-up went on perfectly, and I felt pretty knowing I'd please him if I wore what he asked. Our dinner reservations were for 7:00 P.M. The hostess escorted Gary and I to our table. I was delighted to be dressed up and on an actual date like a normal couple. Too many hours were spent working on our dead–end advancements. Some sweet talk and flirtation with one another might smooth over all the blunders I'd made.

"Thanks for wearing my favorite suit, but I think it's a little tight on you. You might need to lose a few pounds, not many maybe five," Gary's idea of a compliment.

This restaurant was special to us, our first date as a couple. Now we sat in the exact table like once before. The soft music allowed intimate conversation. Small bouquets of fresh flowers on each table along with votive candles added to the romantic ambience, exactly what we needed at this point in our relationship. The candle flames danced inside theirs holders. I hoped our feelings for each other might warm and light a new flame in our hearts. Our spark desperately needed to be relit.

Our spark desperately needed to be relit.

"Here's a little something I thought you'd like, but you can't open it until we get back home." The tiny blue box and fluffy ribbon teased me from the table. He was a great gift giver, especially after some abuse had occurred. It was his way of saying he was sorry, and this present looked intriguing.

"Please? I can't wait that long." I smiled sweetly and batted my eyelashes.

"Let's see you had the medium rare steak, right sir?" The waiter slid the plate in front of Gary.

The moment had passed. I knew I'd have to wait to open the package, encouraged that this night might be tender after all. We laughed at the couple seated across from us and held hands under the table, laughter a huge accomplishment for us. Real food–steak, it had been a long time since I'd enjoyed such luxury, a far more delicious meal than pot pies or bologna sandwiches. My mouth watered in anticipation. I cut into the hunk of meat that sizzled on my plate.

Like a frozen windshield you pour hot water on, the mood was cracked.

"How's your steak, sir?" The waiter inquired.

"Definitely not the way I like it," Gary snapped.

Gary became enraged that the service and food were not up to standard. He berated the waiter, chef, and manager. His steak was returned to the kitchen at no charge; mine was placed in a to–go box. Laughter was over. The blue box was grabbed up and crammed into his pocket. Never to be opened.

We exited the restaurant.

We drove home in silence. Only traffic noises were heard in the westward bound vehicle. He pulled into the driveway and shoved the gearshift into park.

"Get out," he said hatefully.

Chills ran down my spine. I knew my abuser was discontented. Tension oozed from his body. A violent slam of the front door, pictures shook on the wall. He stood in the entryway his fist opened and closed in a strange reflex.

"What are you trying to be? Miss Popularity?" Gary grabbed a fistful of my hair, yanking my neck backward. "Who do you think you are? Flirting with every man in the place like that. You distracted our waiter and he got my steak wrong." He scolded.

"What? You're hurting me. What are you talking about…?" I never finished my defensive statement. He pushed me down the hallway into my bathroom. "No Gary, no," I cried, hands held high into the air in the act of surrender. He soaked a washcloth with cold water and soap and scrubbed my face with sadistic motions calling me every name except my own. Soap saturated my eyes.

Blood seeped from my upper lip from his roughness. Blinded, hurt and in shock, I would have agreed to anything. I was accustomed to his abuse, but this was a new trick in his bag of punishment.

"I've told you," he screamed, "we are together. No one else would have you anyway, so don't get any ideas." Several hard fists landed wherever he could hit. The door slammed. I curled into the corner and sobbed uncontrollably. Obviously, I needed time to think about all the wrongs that just occurred. Instead, all I could think about was what had come of my life. I kept thinking of his eyes. Something was more frightening about the look in his eyes than his actions. In my pain, I couldn't identify the eerie sensation. Anger fled in a second. Then sheer terror overtook me. I had no idea what wrong I committed, but I wasn't about to ask. I'd accept his correction and learn any change he required. I deserved it. I was a failure, but feared that one day he might go too far and try to eliminate the problem. Me. My abuser had enticed, captured, and as a result, I was bound.

"I had no idea what wrong I had committed"

Bound

The next morning I was so stiff and sore I could barely get out of bed. I had to go to work. What I wanted was to go to the hospital and check my ribs, but I couldn't afford to be without a paycheck. Every step, I suffered in silence. My co–workers mustn't know how pitiful a person I am.

"Kerrie, did you oversleep this morning?" a friend asked at lunch time.

"No. Why?"

"I love the way you make up your eyes, but lately you don't wear any makeup. You don't look like yourself."

Her words were fact. I was a stranger to myself. Fortunately, she couldn't see the bruises and scars both inside and outside my body, only my red eyes. My abuser had reestablished the damaged view I saw daily in the reflection of my mirror. The problem. The view of the person that stared back at me had **not** been reformed into a princess. I was definitely the lonely handmaid.

Bound, I found my fate was inevitable–I had to stay with him. No one else would have me. The thought of this devastation the rest of my life, left me completely distraught. Empty. I had to get from beneath his control, somehow, someway.

Several weeks later, I worked up courage. I decided our aggressive relationship had turned vicious, unhealthy, and must end. No matter what the cost. I'd lost everyone in my life, and now ultimately, I had lost myself. Totally. A broken woman with two years of my life wasted, I had to construct a plan of action. I drove the long way to his house while I prepared my speech. Timidly I knocked on his door.

"Come on in. What are you doing here today? I thought you had some places you had to go?" I stepped just inside the doorway, and tried to gather my strength. With downcast eyes I said, "Gary, I'm sorry. I just can't take anymore," I twisted the bangle bracelet on my wrist. "You have too many rules that I can't follow, or keep straight." I whispered.

"What? What are you saying?"

"I'm done – we're over". The look on his face told me he was shocked. Did he realize he had lost control of me?

"What are you trying to say?"

I fought the fear to look him square in the eyes. They frightened me. I couldn't. I played with a loose string on my purse. I managed to pull all the strength from within me. "I…I don't want to be with you anymore."

"You selfish, ungrateful brat. Who made you grow up? Who helped you with money, groceries, bills and made you what you are today? Me. You hear? Me. You can't do anything without me." He lunged for me, grabbing my arm and twisting it until I fell to my knees. "Me. You hear me!" He slapped my face hard. "Don't you think you're ever going to leave me. Ever!" I tried to curl into a ball in self-defense. Slaps and hits came at my body from every direction. Suddenly, like a child's toy with a run-down battery, Gary stopped his hand in mid-slap. A tear ran down his cheek. He wasn't accustomed to any show of strength on my part, only weakness. Maybe that's what made him stop.

"I'm so sorry. I don't know what comes over me. Forgive me?" He covered his eyes with his hands and began to sob.

An apology? Was he really sorry? He saw that I was not going to take any more abuse from him. For whatever reasons, I thought he would change. I conceded.

He promised no more hitting. He'd get control. I fell for his apology, but a cloud of skepticism hung in the air.

I didn't know that he had a plan of his own. A few weeks of peace always followed an apology; the calm before the storm. It seemed Gary had forgiven me for stepping out of line, but my heart ached for my freedom. I was totally blind to the fact he was about to erupt, and nothing compared to his temper. It was a holiday, the Fourth–of–July. We planned to visit his family in a nearby town. I hoped we had bridged our differences.

I waited patiently for the LORD; he turned to me and heard my cry. He lifted me out of the slimy pit, out of the mud and mire; he set my feet on a rock and gave me a firm place to stand. (NIV)

Psalm 40:1-3

Chapter 9

THE BRIDGE INCIDENT

Gary said that Independence Day was his mom's favorite holiday. She loved to watch the grandchildren twirl sparklers, to watch their eyes light up with glee. The climax for the eventful day was always a trip to the fireworks display at the football stadium. She said she loved to see the rockets red glare. Most of all, she loved the food. Hot dogs, ribs, potato salad, chips, dips, and baked beans–down home cooking she called it. I enjoyed meeting her and looked forward to becoming better acquainted.

His family seemed much like mine, divided into two groups. The talkers and the TV nuts. The talkers sat in groups and recalled the days of yesteryear, vacations, and swapped recipes. The TV nuts sat in front of the television and dreamed of bygone days when they could carry the ball and run fast. Their memories probably exceeded their abilities.

My hands went cold.

It looked as if Gary's Mom had prepared the meal for days. A real smorgasbord sat on every table, shelf, and cabinet. The guests feasted and left a mess large enough to require two dishwasher loads, even though paper plates had been used.

One couple stood off to the side. They avoided the family talks and fun. When I commented about them, Gary corrected me immediately.

"You don't stick your nose into things that don't concern you," he barked in my face and squeezed my arm hard. "We'll talk about this when we get home."

My hands went cold. I realized I'd broken two rules– an opinion and a question. He stomped back into the house, leaving me reprimanded and ashamed in front of his relatives.

"Get in the car," he demanded upon his return. "We're leaving."

"But I haven't said goodbye or anything to your mom or anyone."

"She knows–no need to embarrass me further. And can't you just once do as I ask you?" he said between clenched teeth.

The traffic was sparse on the highway. Dark–thirty - time for fireworks. We headed in the opposite direction of Roman candles that exploded in the black, starlit sky. Gary stared straight ahead at the road. His jaw muscles flexed; his knuckles paled from his tight grip on the steering wheel. I knew to be silent.

He turned the car off the usual route home into unfamiliar territory. Silence. I hated when he was quiet. Why do I keep messing up? Fear consumed me.

Slowly he brought the car to a stop underneath a bridge. He rolled down the windows, his glare straight ahead into the shadows of the night. Crickets chirped in serene harmony for a few seconds; their fast shrills matched my rapid heartbeats. I was frightened because I knew this wasn't the way home. His stone cold face was a visual clue. His fury was about to erupt. The thump of tires from an occasional car driving on the overhead bridge echoed above us. Hot, summer night breezes turned icy cold. He turned off the ignition key and slid across the seat. His arm slithered around my shoulder. His eyes became small evil slits, as he turned to glare at me.

"You know, I could kill you right now, and not a soul in this world would care." His hot breath warmed the frost of fear deep inside me. He grabbed my upper arms in a vise grip.

"You have no friends, and even your parents think you're worthless." He shook my shoulders with brutal rage.

"It would take days for people to even notice you were missing." He said, his eyebrows raised.

His demeaning words "worthless" and "no one would care" rang true to my very core. Astonished, I knew he was exactly right. I had heard the disparaging list of who Kerrie was, long enough.Who would care? Me? I didn't any more.

A brutal shove. I lay flat. Gary straddled me, mounting his full weight on my chest.

"I could kill you." His eyes darted from side–to-side. The eyes were familiar. I had seen this look before. Where had I seen that look? My mind searched the past. Memories like cobwebs. The eyes…

Oh God – I was four-years-old again.

Strong large hands wrapped around my throat. Slow, even pressure closed my windpipe. A sea of gray engulfed Gary's silhouette. Green neon lights danced in front of my closed eyelids. Reflexes for survival swarmed my spirit. Coughing, gasping. I opened my eyes to look into my assailant's face; a demon held my life in his hands.

I recognized the eyes of the avenger.

The eyes I'd seen in my haven!

The corner!

Mom's piano!

The vacant, evil eyes of a killer.

God help me, my numb brain screamed silently.

His knees pressed my ribs into my lungs. Black fog covered my eyes. Gasping, I whispered, "J-u-s-t. d-o. i-t." My skull felt like it would explode. I sank deeper into murky fog.

Afraid of the "D" words no longer. I craved death - it *had* to be better.

The pastor's words echoed in my memory of a promised hero. Jesus Christ.

The prayer of salvation. Heaven. Something had to remove my pain. The hero held the key.

Something had to unlock the pain. The hero must have the key.

"Please, just do it." The words tumbled out of my mouth. He knew he had accomplished what he had set out to do. He had conquered me.

I had pleaded. He denied me the satisfaction.

My spirit had died long ago. Only my body would be found under the bridge. Gary would gain nothing from my murder. He withheld what I craved.

Death.

Consciousness left me. I spiraled into black oblivion.

Defiled like never before. Dirty to my inner core. I awoke in the soggy mud of my front lawn. The slow, constant swish of the automatic water sprinkler spouted cool water high into the air. I looked through half-opened, blurred eyes.

In the very early hours of the next day, I wondered *were these my tears, or rain.*

Vaguely I remembered Gary yanked me by my ankles. He dumped me from the front seat of his car onto my lawn. I lay in the muck and the mire like a bag of discarded rubbish. I tried to move. My throat, head, and every bone throbbed with pain. A can rolled down the sidewalk and fell with a clank onto the step. Another roll of the can dropped to the step lower. *Clank* I felt the chain of death drag behind me as I crawled on hands and knees. "God, please help me," I murmured. It wasn't even a real prayer, just a statement.

Was it the wetness of the grass?

Soft Mud?

Something soft and unearthly sweet seemed to caress my cheek. Was it the hand of the Lord that touched me?

I crawled across the wet grass, unlocked my door, and fell inside my apartment. I heaved myself onto the couch. A light came on in the dark of my soul.

That day was a defining moment in my life, and so is this one. Uncertain then about eternity, now as I lay here in the MRI tube, I *know* I would go to heaven, but the hurtful realization seeped into my spirit: I do not have a real relationship with Jesus.

You prepare a table before me in the presence of my enemies…

That's an understatement. I had been at the table, living and doing life with my enemy. He had stolen everything from me, and I had let him. My abuser made me believe the worst about myself. He came to steal, kill, and destroy my identity. Escaping from that relationship was the hardest and best thing I ever did. Sometimes, even today, I look over my shoulder to see if my enemy has found me, and ready to fulfill the promise that he made long ago. Independence Day was when I received my freedom, in more ways than one.

"Five more minutes Mrs. Oles. You're doing well." Roberta startled me as her voice jumped through my headphones.

. . . *"Get me out of here,"* I wanted to yell. *"I can't take anymore."* It had nothing to do with the MRI test–just my past.

Every loud clank had been the symbolization of all the chains I had dragged for years; a girl shackled to her past. I longed to exchange my life for someone else's – anyone's – but mine.

"Therefore I say to you, her sins, which are many, are forgiven..."

Luke 7:47

Chapter 10

THE EXCHANGE

An exchange was made under the bridge that night - death for life. Years of abuse now a distant memory; I still wasn't aware of my true identity. From the depths of my soul I ached, and I no longer cared what the results of the test were going to be. My life had been a tattered mess. Though the tormenting memories have faded, I couldn't escape the relevant pictures, of the chains of my past.

You anoint my head with oil; my cup runs over.

As the movie of my youth and young adulthood came to an end, I wondered if my tears might interfere with the MRI results. Then the slightest glimpse of hope arose as I thought about how Psalm 23 had somehow fit into my troubled life.

The scripture and my memories were there side-by-side in the clanking tube. God's word had pinpointed the chains that bound me, and I realized I had dressed myself up for life, but I had never been free from the chains.

I prayed silently, *God heal me, and I promise I will make my life different. I'll try to live for you. I can't do this thing called life on my own. If you lead me, I will follow.*

I heard the words, "My child." The voice of my heavenly Father said, "You are healed." It seemed, for the first time in my life, I heard the silent, soothing voice of God. He called me His child! The words washed over me, and warmth covered my cold, shivering body. Calmness. Inner peace came immediately.

At times I had been skeptical of those who said they had heard God. I knew I had heard him clearly.

He had heard my plea, and I knew I was loved. God had rescued me many times before, but I hadn't always realized it. This time, there was no mistake.

The seemingly unending MRI clanks finally ended, and the conveyor belt delivered me like a newborn out of the canal. I was a new creation.

It was ME.

Something had come to life inside the tube - it was ME. I was still blind, but I had never seen more clearly.

"How are you doing, kid?" Roberta's upbeat voice asked.

"Actually, I am going to be okay."

"Can you see?" she asked excitedly.

Tears rolled from the corners of my eyes and dripped into my ears. "No, but I will soon."

The same cheery voiced person who delivered me to the MRI test earlier, rolled me back to my room on a non-wobbly gurney. Life was already smoother.

"Here we are back to your room again, Mrs. Oles." Her cheery voice was now a comfort rather than the irritation I felt before.

"Hi Babe, that didn't take long." Phillip helped me onto my bed and fluffed my pillow.

I thought it had been a lifetime.

"I'm so glad you're here. You kept your promise. I have so much to tell you. You'll never believe what all happened."

"Can you see?" he asked the same aggravating question.

"No, but let me tell you what I learned."

Knowing in the depths of my soul God had saved a wretch like me. I described to Phillip my life's journey through the MRI tube, every painful hurt, fear, and episode. Still lying in the blurred, darkness; we both began to see the light.

That afternoon Mom and Dad brought my children to the hospital. Family members and friends waited to hear the doctor's report. When the neurologist came into my room, he began with sorrow in his voice.

"Kerrie, I'm going to release you today. I cannot find anything on any test. They are all negative or normal. We've been at this for days."

"It's okay," I interrupted the sorrowful voice, "God said He'd heal me."

"Can you see?" I heard skepticism in his voice.

"No, but that's all right, I believe I will soon." I gave glory to God for the first time. The doctor left the room.

I felt Caleb's small tender hand on mine. "Mommy, what did that man say to you?"

"He said I can come home to you."

"Oh goodie, Mommy," he hugged my hand. I reached to caress his face. "I prayed to Jesus to make you see. He told me He would help you."

I don't know where he learned that, but I squeezed him tight, "Thank you, baby."

I knew I had to have Caleb's same childlike faith.

Three days, no results, doctors stumped, and forty–five minutes in the second MRI tube, my life was changed. Released from the hospital into freedom!

The Dwelling Place

Surely goodness and mercy shall follow me all the days of my life…and I will dwell in the house of the Lord forever...

The drive home was certainly going to be different than the ride to the hospital. Fear and horror had accompanied me in my Dad's car, but I departed for home with faith and hope as my new companions for new destinations.

Phillip buckled Cameron into his car seat, "You guys ready to take Mommy home?"

"Let's go home," Caleb said, kicking his feet against the back of my seat.

"We'll play I Spy." Phillip started the car. "I spy something red," he said.

"I know, I know. The red light. R-e-d means stop," Caleb said.

"Very good, Caleb."

"My time. I spy something with my little eye that has toys," he giggled.

"I know we're driving by Toys R Us."

"That's right, Mommy."

How like my sweet boys to help me know our locations in route to home. I wasn't lost in darkness – I was headed in the right direction.

"Daddy," I said, "you're very sweet to Mommy." I blew him a kiss. Life felt somewhat normal on the dark, blurred drive.

Our SUV came to a stop. "We're home, honey. I'll get Cameron. He's fast asleep, and I'll come back for you. Okay?" I heard Phillip's seatbelt slide backward. "Caleb, stay here with Mommy." The car door shut.

My first test. I had to believe I'd see my boys again. Somehow I had to take a step of faith.

"Caleb, Mommy has an idea. Let's play train. You can be the engineer and I'll be the caboose. I'll hold on to your shoulders, and you can lead me inside to the kitchen."

"Okay. Choo-choo. Here comes the train." He shuffled his feet. "Choo-choo."

I held his shoulders and scooted along with my small engineer, all the time thinking – *childlike faith. I can make it.*

Phillip's footsteps were heavy as he hurried down the stairs. "Well, how did you get inside?"

"I helped, Daddy. We played train."

"Good boy, Caleb. You're Mommy's big helper."

Phillip scooped me up into his strong arms. "I'll carry you up the stairs. I think you need a nap." He kissed my check with tenderness.

My darkness felt different; I even felt physically lighter, more aware of my surroundings. Aromatic smells of fresh flowers filled the house. Phillip lowered me onto our bed. Clean, crisp sheets that smelled of vanilla fabric softener comforted my body. The slow tick of the wall clock and four chimes. Four o'clock, a great hour for a nap. My house was now a home to me. Mom's thoughtful touches of lemon oil furniture spray, Pine Sol, and freshness tantalized my senses. Exhausted, I slept deeply.

The clock chimed six. I looked at the alarm clock, next to the bed…five-fifty. I need to set the wall clock; it's fast again. Phillip's suitcases set in the corner, his business suit draped over the top. *I'll have to take that to the cleaners. Gosh, I need to fix dinner.*

What was happening? I rubbed my eyes in shock. Five–fifty one.

"Phillip!" I yelled. "Phillip! Come quick." I heard him take two stairs at a time.

He ran into the room, a two-day stubble growth covered his face, and dark circles framed his eyes, worry and stress visible on his handsome face. He carried Cameron on his hip. Milk dripped from Cameron's upside-down sippy-cup and chin. His tiny hand held a chocolate chip cookie.

"Mommy," Caleb said as he reached out for me, "can I have some chocolate milk?"

"Come here to Mommy." He ran to the side of my bed. I licked my thumb and wiped peanut butter from his cheek. "Doesn't Daddy know how to wash your face? You've got jelly and peanut butter from ear to ear."

As our eyes of childlike faith met, I realized Caleb knew I could see. He jumped into my arms. We hugged and giggled. My three loves and I cried, rolled and giggled on the bed. Finally exhausted with joy and needing to memorize my gifts from God, I caressed each face, outlining their noses, eyes, and lips.

It was a while before I learned; I had received grace into my heart at the end of those three days. Life came full circle. I began to discover God loved me, not because of anything I did or didn't do. He loved me because of His grace. It is truly amazing. I not only discovered that about God, but I discovered I longed to be with Him in a way I had never before.

I talked to God for hours - and He listened.

Late that night, my three loves fast asleep, I found my secret hiding place. Now accustomed to the dark, no longer afraid to be alone, I knelt in my closet to finish the Psalm.

And I will dwell in the house of the Lord forever.

Not knowing how to pray, I talked to God for hours – and He listened.

I exchanged invisible chains that shackled me to my past for a life of freedom. That day in the MRI tube, I met a new man – the only man that could fill the void in my life. I had settled for counterfeit relationships for years. I met the genuine Redeemer inside the tube. His name is Jesus, He lives within me, and I exchanged my agenda for His.

Grateful for His grace, I now belonged to the greater one.

They overcame him by the blood of the Lamb and by the word of their testimony.

Revelation 12:11

FROM MY HEART...
GRACE-FULL LIVING

The purpose for writing this book was to share my heart's burden. I have great empathy for those who are physically blind, but even more for those who are spiritually blind.

Spiritual blindness is the failure to understand, receive, and live out God's unconditional grace. Within the pages of *Invisible Chains,* I'm sure you saw my spiritual blindness. I am often asked, "Are you afraid you will lose your sight again?"

I never want that to happen, but it *was* the pivotal point in my life. The affliction caused me to look with different sight to God. I learned to receive His grace.

Grace is defined as God's free and unmerited favor toward sinful humanity. We are the sinful humanity, but by His grace we are forgiven. It's His free gift to us!

I may have been saved by grace, but I hadn't really received it into my heart, because I didn't believe I deserved it. You may think the same way. Do you visualize God with a scale measuring the good and the bad you have done? The bad will always outweigh the good, because we live in a fallen world. I didn't believe God could love me because of all the bad things on the scale. I carried that thinking for years. ***Those*** were the chains that bound me: the chains of my past.

We are a nation lost to our pasts.

We are a nation lost to our pasts. Our pasts keep us from our present and our purpose.

Chained by "who we were," we can never move into "who we are called to be."

Phillip Yancey, the author of the book *What's So Amazing about Grace?*, wrote a powerful quote. "Grace does not excuse sin, but it treasures the sinner."

Do you believe YOU are a treasure to the Heavenly Father?

Go back with me to your childhood school days. Remember making a poster board collage. Pasting pictures that described something about us on a board, while others guessed who the board belonged to. In our adulthood, we are walking poster boards. The collage of our life is pasted on us: circumstances, trials, tragedies, and successes have attached themselves to the pages of our lives, and they become our identity; they are just invisible.

Those were some of the names used to describe me that I've carried on my invisible collage. How could God treasure me? By His amazing grace!

If any of these names have you bound, my friend, then this book was written for you. Jesus wants you free from those false identities, and wants you to come into agreement with Him on how He sees you. He knows the worst about us but sees our best.

Despite whatever the pages of your life have been, the truth is YOU are treasured too.

When you begin to doubt God's grace or question His love, I encourage you to open the beautiful pages of scripture. As you read about the kinds of people Jesus showed His grace and love to, it will plant the truth in your heart and give you a renewed sense of hope.

Allow me to point out a few of God's people:

- Rahab - first introduced as a harlot, and became a life redeemed.
- The Samaritan woman - had multiple husbands, but found the water of life.
- Jacob - a man who dared to wrestle with God.
- Apostle Paul - an apostle of grace. He was recruited from the ranks of the Christian torturers, to a servant of Jesus, and would ultimately be known as the greatest missionary in all of history.

When I read about their lives, it restored my faith that God could really love me too.

As I wrote my story, the girl on each page seemed like a stranger, because the Bible says in Romans 6:11 that all the things I had done are dead!

In the same way, count yourselves dead to sin but alive to God in Christ Jesus.

What a great indication of how He feels about you and me. He knew every wrong thing we were ever going to do, and He still sent His son to die for *all of them*.

What happened to me inside the MRI tube is I became aware that I no longer had to carry the chains of my past. Jesus had already taken them. I needed to let them go.

My eyes may have been healed, but there was a full miracle in my heart!

For many years, I lived "far off" from God. This does not mean distance; it refers to the state of my soul. I longed for relationship. I calculated that I lived 13,680 days "far off" from Him. Since this life is only preparation for our eternal home, I don't want to live one day without walking in a real relationship with Him.

I finally know that He doesn't love me based on my past; He loves me out of His Grace. People from all cultures, denominations, and every corner of the world can relate to not knowing the love of the Father, and my heart breaks for them.

Where are you today, as you read this book? If you answered that you still struggle in knowing you are loved, keep this acronym in mind:

Focus on the Father, not on the things of this world, to fill the voids in your life

Receive the grace that is offered freely to you by God

Engage yourself in a relationship with Jesus; spend time with Him and the Word

Evolve into who you were created to be

If you have never accepted Christ as your personal Savior, or you need a renewed sense of grace, I invite you to say this prayer with me:

Heavenly Father, I invite you to come into my heart. I've been hiding my pain for far too long, and I desire to have a personal relationship with you. I ask by your grace that you unlock all the chains of my past that have weighed me down. Please forgive my sins, Jesus. I believe you are the only one who can fill me. I ask you to be my Lord and Savior. Thank you for your forgiveness, for your grace, and your love that will never fail.

In Jesus name I pray, Amen.

As you've read my story, I pray you have found your own. I urge you to ask Him for the key of grace to unlock your chains. Receive, and begin to walk in His love and freedom.

There is no time like the present to do away with your past!

I pray you will walk in a "grace-full life," – **never to drag your chains again!**

This will be written for the generation to come, that a people yet to be created may praise the LORD.

Psalm 102:18

FROM A MOTHER'S HEART

A child is truly one of the greatest gifts from God. I was blessed beyond all expectations when I gave birth to a baby girl I named Kerrie. Like all mothers, I feel my child is smart, beautiful, and exceptional.

I protected her from falls when she learned to walk, from hot stoves when she was a toddler, from strangers when she played outside, and from cars when we crossed streets. I comforted her when she was sad, applied bandages when she skinned her knee, and sat up with her when she was sick.

When she became a woman, I had to let go. When she needed me, I was there. But there were times I didn't know about her pain. In fact, I learned much during the writing of this book, and my heart ached.

As a co–author of this book, I had to write in my daughter's point of view. POV is hard to learn and write properly. Basically, the person on paper can only see, talk, feel and explain what they are seeing, feeling, and thinking. They cannot feel other people's reactions. To place myself inside my daughter's emotions challenged me as a writer and a mother. I lived this book, and her life, twice: once through the pain of a mother's experience, and again through hers. You may find some pages still damp from this mother's tears. The experience, however difficult, was phenomenal. I challenge you to take a hurtful experience of your child, write his or her feelings, not yours, and feel the outcome.

Living my daughter's pains, dragging her invisible chains, I found my own chains as well. A cleansing took place in my life via this heart–wrenching experience. I pray that your chains that may have you bound will be revealed to you. When analyzing the love of a mother, I reflected on our heavenly Father's love. He must hurt for His children when we fail to partake of His blessings. One rainy day while writing a chapter, I wondered, *maybe, rain isn't just to soften the hard dry ground. Maybe rain is the Father's tears, crying for His children. Yet, via rain–things grow, and a harvest will come.*

ACKNOWLEDGEMENTS

Kerrie would like to thank:

My husband Phillip for being an example of a Godly man by leading me and our family, and for your love and support that has never wavered; My mom, Olivia and dad, Joe, for taking this journey with me of writing my story and for always loving me past all my mistakes; A special thanks to Paul and Judi Cole for your vision and support of this project, and for your wonderful friendship; Russell Lake at Seed Studios for being led by the Lord and bringing to fruition the publishing of my story, you made a life very changed; Jennifer Lake for your time and keen eye on the edits; and to each and every friend that has supported, prayed for, and encouraged me in the "thing" that's mine to do in the kingdom!

Olivia would like to thank:

Joe, my husband of forty-five years, for making life worthwhile, fun, and for your support in everything I've attempted in life. You've made life an adventure; Thanks to all the authors of the North Texas Christian Writers Association for their suggestions and teachings over the years; a special thanks to LaWanda Bailey, my best friend, who encouraged me when I wanted to give up on many issues in life. Without your assistance, this book would not have been completed.

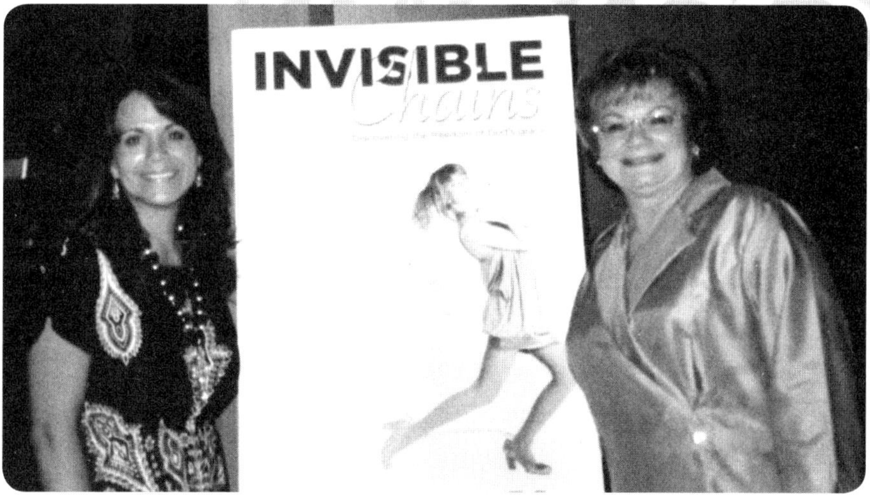